IS

GW01401149

1. The beginning of everything

Most people believe that all things progressed from the simplest organisms to the most complex, over many millions of years by slow step-by-step changes.

A little under two hundred years ago some scientists, studying nature and the rocks and fossils, concluded that all the stars and planets—including Planet Earth—must be many millions, even billions, of years old. They suggested that everything slowly evolved from simple to complex. Today, many scientists believe that a sudden Big Bang in space kick-started everything, and from there things 'evolved' slowly. Very, very slowly. This is the 'theory of evolution'.

There are two immediate problems with this idea:

First, it starts part way through the story. For example, explaining how creatures with better eyesight had a better chance of survival, doesn't explain how light-sensitive cells, lenses, and all the electrical wiring from eye to brain started in the first place. The story is told of the man who boasted to God: 'I too can make man out of a handful of dust.' God replied, 'Go ahead then.' So, the man reached out and took a handful of dust. God suddenly interrupted: 'Hold on, go and get your own dust.'

Second, it demands blind faith in unimaginable odds. No scientist has ever seen these billions of detailed and vital changes happening so that after millions of years one kind of thing develops into another very different kind of thing—like a blob of something becoming a fishlike thing and eventually an elephant.

Evolution is called 'a theory'. A theory is a suggested explanation which is not yet proven. But evolution isn't treated like that. Many scientists are sure it is proven, and most people today believe in evolution as a fact because they are told it is. But evolution depends on lots of unproved ideas.

Here's something every honest scientist should admit: science doesn't know *for sure* how life on Planet Earth started. There are plenty of ideas: A big cosmic bang, a primordial soup, a hydrothermal vent, an asteroid or comet from outer space—each with its variations. But not one can be presented as fact and, as we said, each one starts part way through the story. Every idea starts with stuff somewhere—but who knows where all the original 'stuff' came from?

2. Science and scientists

Science is the careful study and testing of everything around us in the natural world. Scientists are those who take on this study and testing and then come to conclusions.

Science provides the building blocks for scientists to work with. All scientists work with the same building blocks, though they may come to very different conclusions.

There is *observational science*, which is what we see and experiment with.

There is *historical science*, which is how we interpret what we see in the present world to understand what may have happened in the past.

Much of historical science *assumes* what is called *naturalism*: which means that everything that happens now and happened in the past is the result of natural causes that scientists think they can explain. The possibility of the supernatural, like miracles, is ruled out. Naturalism also *assumes* that what we observe happening today is the same as has always been happening: the present is the key to the past. *These two assumptions—* scientists can explain everything, and things have always been happening as they are now—*can be seriously wrong and skew a scientist's conclusions*. Keep this in mind.

A few more things to remember:

Scientists are not infallible. Scientists come to conclusions that may be right or wrong. Scientific conclusions are frequently changing. None of us would want to be treated today by an 18th century doctor!

Scientific conclusions must always be open to change.
In 1847 a young Hungarian doctor, Ignaz Semmelweis, insisted that doctors in his maternity wards in Vienna must wash their hands between examinations of expectant mothers. He was ridiculed by the profession, but the mortality rate in his hospital fell dramatically from one in six to one in eighty-four. We can rarely say, 'Science proves …'. At best we can only say, 'Today most scientists believe …'.

Evolution may be presented as 'an accepted theory', but it involves too many assumptions to be taken as a fact. We should always be allowed to question it and suggest alternatives. That is how science progresses.

Unbiased science is not easy. What we hope to find (a presupposition) can often affect how we interpret what we see. For example, *Naturalism* will never allow for the possibility of the supernatural. In the media and education, challenges to the theory of evolution should always be allowed, otherwise we have closed our minds to the possibility of a theory being wrong. Only false theories need protecting from an alternative.

Scientific experiments must be ready to discover the unacceptable

3. What did Darwin believe?

In 1859 Charles Darwin published *On the Origin of Species by Means of Natural Selection* and in 1871 *The Descent of Man, and Selection in relation to sex.*

Most people have heard of Darwin's first book but have never heard of the second. *The Descent of Man* was even more significant. He presented the idea of all things evolving slowly with only the fittest surviving, and that humans were descended from ape-like creatures. He admitted there were no fossil or bone skeletons of missing links, but concluded: 'No one will lay much stress on this fact.' *Missing links* would be a major piece of evidence, but the absence of it didn't seem to matter to Darwin!

Darwin thought that the key to evolution was the similarity in mammals, birds, reptiles, amphibians and fish. They each have a lot in common. That hardly proves evolution. Aeroplanes and submarines have a lot in common but that is no evidence they all emerged from the same production line.

Darwin's assumption was that all forms of life on earth descended from 'some fishlike animal'. That is what most evolutionists believe today. But that is completely unproven. There is no evidence for that theory.

Keep in mind the distinction between a 'kind' and a 'species'. A 'kind' is a separate type of animal (like horse and giraffe). A 'species' is a difference within a 'kind' (like zebra and pony). Animals of different but related 'species' can often interbreed with each other, but those of one 'kind' cannot interbreed with those of a different 'kind'.

Darwin considered humans are only a higher form of the animal world. Our bigger brain size means we have come out on top. Because the success of evolution is dependent on the survival of the fittest, Darwin referred to superior and inferior races. He referred to Aboriginals, black people and pygmies as 'barbarians', 'degraded' and 'savages' (a word used over 120 times in *The Descent of Man*). He compared them to 'lower' organisms. Darwin concluded: 'At some future period ... the civilised races of man will almost certainly exterminate and replace the savage races throughout the world.'

Darwin's principle of higher and lower races and the survival of the fittest has led to much human suffering. For example, Hitler's view of a 'superior race' was based on Darwin and led to the holocaust. Slavery, 'racial' discrimination, and the killing of unwanted babies are also consistent with his idea of evolution. It disposes of those who are considered inferior and would therefore threaten the survival (or convenience) of the fit.

It was the Darwinian theories of superior races that led to the holocaust of Hitler's Third Reich and recent 'ethnic cleansing'

4. The Big Start

The 'Big Bang' is presented as if it was a certain scientific fact. It is only one of many theories.

This theory is that the universe began as a tiny dot of nothing or something! One moment, around fourteen billion years ago, it exploded, and it has been expanding ever since. This original idea of Georges Lemaitre in 1927 has been added to by Edwin Hubble and others. It is known as *Hubble's Law*. It's only an idea without any evidence.

Other scientists reject the big bang and offer alternatives. Fred Hoyle's 'Steady State' theory is one, and Carlo Rovelli's 'Big Bounce' is another. Even the suggestion of multi-universes, once the idea of science fiction writers, is now openly discussed by cosmologists (those who study the history of the universe). Various ideas and huge assumptions have to be made. In cosmology very little is certain; even the existence of 'black holes' is challenged.

There are many problems with the Big Bang theory. It depends upon dark matter and dark energy; dark matter has been discovered but dark energy, which is thought to make up around 70% of the universe, is acknowledged to be 'a complete mystery'. None has been found. Also, the rate at which everything grew in those seconds after the bang is simply speculation—as is the fourteen billion years.

Whatever theory fits best, significant preexisting 'stuff' is always necessary, and the actual way in which this cosmic dot 'of infinite density' expanded demands a number of suggestions, theories and presuppositions. Even the famous Stephen Hawking changed his view more than once. It is admitted by all honest scientists that it is still only an idea with many critics. No one saw or has discovered the Big Bang. It is an assumption and should never be written or spoken of as a fact of science.

If a miracle is defined as an event that cannot be explained by any known natural cause, all scientists believe in miracles. Because whatever theory they have for the origin of the universe, they are left with the miracle that it all started from nothing. Oxford Professor Peter Atkins suggests that the universe is 'an elaborate and engaging rearrangement of nothing'—so he presumably believes that something *can* come from nothing. That's a miracle.

5. Designer labels and DNA

Right from the start, all known creatures have a perfect and complete set of instructions for their development, function, growth and reproduction—this is the human *genome*.

The genome is made up of an amazing information store of molecules known as DNA (deoxyribonucleic acid) which contains these instructions. DNA teams up with RNA (ribonucleic acid) that reads the DNA codes and kick-starts the process of development and growth. Put simply (and it's really very complex), the full DNA information of all living things is coded-in right from the start. If some information is lost or altered (it's called a 'mutation') the result is mostly harmful; *never* is a new 'kind' formed. One thing is sure: nothing is *ever* added. All scientists agree with this. This is the designer label that marks out one thing (kind) from another.

DNA is stored in chromosomes, and in our human genome there are twenty-three pairs of chromosomes. Half come from the father and half from the mother. That's why we all show features of both our parents.

Think of your body as a huge and complicated building with hundreds of thousands of detailed parts—actually, the human genome has at least three billion bits of information. Before the construction company can start work, they must have detailed instructions from the architect, engineers and surveyors so they know how everything fits together. No one assumes the building just 'happened' accidentally or the builders made it up bit by bit as they went along. So, how did all our DNA information and instructions get there?

All around us we see design. Everyone agrees that if there is a smart creation (car, building, dress, picture and so on) there must be a smart designer. We accept, without question, that the more complex the creation, the more intelligent and creative the designer.

Nothing, anywhere in all creation is more complex than you.

In all observable science—no exceptions—when a sperm (male) meets an egg (female), all the information for what follows is coded in the DNA of both parents. Another thing is certain: only an individual of the same kind (goat, human, fish, etc.) will result. There will be minor differences—no two individuals are ever truly identical—but *always* they are the same kind. Scientists have *never* observed a new kind emerging. So, on the basis of the evolutionary rule that the present is the key to

the past, there is *no scientific evidence of one kind becoming another different kind.*

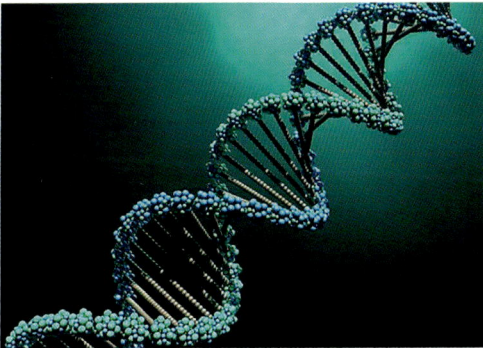

A strand of DNA—design always involves a designer

6. Apes to humans—really?

It is so common to be told that we all evolved from creatures like chimpanzees that you might be forgiven for thinking it's true.

Darwin's starting point for evolution was the similarity between animals and humans. He assumed that things like arms, legs, hands and feet, proved that all evolved from one common ancestor. But similarities tell you nothing about relationship, only about function and purpose. Frogs also have arms, legs, hands and feet.

So, let's look at the idea that humans evolved from chimpanzees (part of the ape family). There are some obvious similarities. However, chimpanzees and humans are totally different from top to toe—literally.

At the top we have the brain. With its 100 billion cells and 100 trillion connections, the brain to body ratio is five times greater in humans than in apes. Think of the brain power of humans for memory, multi-tasking, analysis, design and engineering, creativity in art and music, reasoning, complex language and much more.

And apes? They have just about learned to smash nuts with a stone and poke out termites with a stick! No scientist has any idea how an ape's brain can evolve into the infinite complexity of the human brain. Arguments that link the size of a skull with brain size are misleading. Modern humans have different size skulls without it affecting their intelligence.

At the bottom we have the foot, which is an entirely different construction in the ape. And the big toe? In humans it is hard and stiff because it is a firm platform for upright walking, jumping and running; in the ape it is an opposite toe, flexible for gripping branches.

Everything in between the top and the toe is different in apes and humans. The whole structure of the skeleton is different. Apes are quadruped (walking on four legs) and humans are biped (two legs). It's not a matter of one slowly learning to stand up straight; the whole bone, joint and ligament structure has to be different to start with. You can't convert a bike into a car; you have to start again.

It is also assumed that humans (they call us *Homo erectus*) were around at least 250,000 years ago. Significantly, the earliest evidence from archaeology for the use of the wheel, which is the easiest and most useful of all tools, only goes back to less than 5,000 years. That should tell us roughly when humans started on earth.

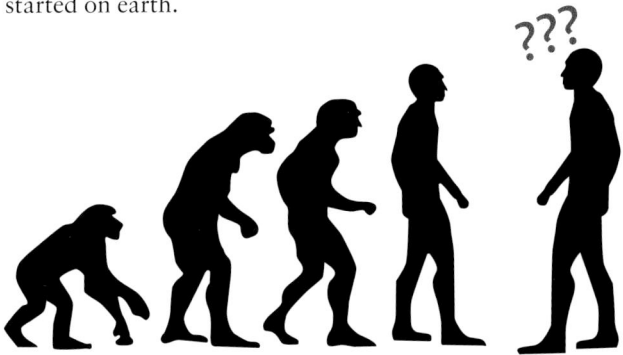

This well-known 'progression' is a myth of evolutionary theory—no such sequence has ever been discovered
(Tkgd2007, CC BY-SA 3.0, Wikimedia Commons)

7. Missing links

No scientist has yet found the 'missing links' that would show a clear progression from primitive to complex.

Drawings of apes developing into humans over millions of years are simply imagination. One researcher wrote: 'Bones are fickle. Bones will sing any song you want to hear.' We have no complete skeletons that show apes developing into humans. Most claims come from just a few bones scattered here and there. The drawings of complete creatures are artists' imagination. From a handful of jigsaw pieces can you really be certain of the complete picture?

Hoax and errors have contributed to the false idea of apes to humans. The infamous Piltdown Man was a hoax. In 1922 the Nebraska Man was based on one tooth and was 'proof' of a missing link—until scientists agreed it belonged to a pig! Neanderthal Man, also proclaimed as the missing link, is now agreed to have been fully human.

Today there are large differences between humans across the world in size and shape of the skeleton, but they are all totally unlike apes which have an entirely different bone and joint structure. Apes to man is a complete myth.

By the way, don't be fooled by the fact that apes share 98% DNA with humans, we share about the same with pigs, and 60% with bananas! This has nothing whatever to do with evolutionary relationships.

Archaeopteryx was once thought to be a missing link between dinosaurs and bird flight. However, since its discovery in 1861 many other bird fossils are found earlier than *Archaeopteryx*. *Archaeopteryx* is clearly just an extinct creature.

The live *Coelacanth* fish caught off the coast of South Africa in 1938 was identical to those known only by fossils in rocks supposedly 70 million years old. It shows no sign of evolution. It's the same with many other animals and insects whose fossils are exactly like the versions we see today. No examples from fossils or skeletons show a creature on the way to becoming something entirely different.

Natural selection and ***adaptation*** are **not** evolution. They are simply natural changes within a species. There are countless examples where the less able or less well camouflaged are eliminated or where adaptation preserves them. The variations in Darwin's finches from the Galapagos Islands are mainly in the beak; they are still finches that interbreed. The differences between humans—the colour of skin, hair and eyes, shape of the face, tone of voice, size, etc.—are no evidence of evolution.

DNA information can be lost, but it is *never* added for one 'kind' to become something different.

This is 'Lucy', a supposed 'missing link'. Compare the bones, which is all we have, with the imaginative drawing of her!

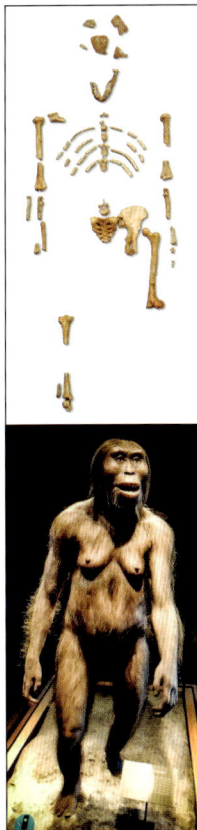

8. Irreducible complexity and impossible mysteries

For things to work properly, every part has to be both present and in good shape; if something is missing, it just won't work.

This **irreducible complexity** is well-known from engineering to biology. Things cannot function unless they are complete. An airliner needs every detail of its engine and superstructure to be in place and working perfectly before it can take off. A part-evolved brain, eye, or ear would be useless. With a part-evolved wing, a dragonfly, bee or butterfly would die. Pluck two leading wing feathers from a bird and it is grounded. This is an unsolved challenge to evolution.

Evolutionists are reluctant to discuss sex! It has been called the 'Queen of problems in evolutionary biology'. We are asked to accept the unbelievable coincidence that somehow virtually all living things evolved two from each kind, a male and a female, that are similar but very different, and are each essential for the survival of that kind—and they evolved separately at exactly the same time and rate, without needing each other until they were fully evolved!

Because some plants are self-fertile, a few scientists, struggling to find a solution, have suggested that long ago a massive alteration (a mutation) in something that could reproduce itself (no one knows what) led to the two sexes. They admit there is zero scientific evidence for this. That's fairy tale, not science.

Impossible mysteries

Think of a butterfly. A small worm-like creature with lots of legs eats only leaves until its skin gets harder and harder. One day it tucks away in a corner, or hangs from a twig, until its skin is hard and shiny. Then it *dissolves into a 'caterpillar soup'* inside its case. This is called a chrysalis. A few weeks later it breaks out as a beautiful creature with wings, that cannot eat leaves but sips nectar from flowers, mates with another of the same species (but the other sex) then lays eggs—and out comes a new caterpillar ...

No one can explain how caterpillar to butterfly via chrysalis 'evolved'. This is acknowledged as 'a genuine biological mystery even today'. Every small detail of the process has to be in place from the start or else—no butterfly or caterpillar.

The so-called 'evolution' of irreducible complexity produces impossible mysteries that are all around you. That's a real problem for evolution because the only alternative is a Designer-Creator, with the DNA instructions being complete to start with.

Life-cycle of the Monarch butterfly

9. Dates for everything

According to the American Space Agency (NASA) the universe is supposedly nearly 14 billion years old and Planet Earth a mere 4.54 billion years. How do we know?

Radioactive (radiometric) dating. Rocks formed from volcanic eruptions (*igneous rocks*) contain many radioactive minerals; the rate of the release of their radiation (radioactive decay) can be measured. This cannot be performed on *sedimentary rocks* which are laid down by water or volcanic ash and cover around three quarters of the earth's surface. However, igneous rock lies beneath most of earth's sedimentary rock. Sedimentary rocks are generally dated by nearby igneous rocks.

However, scientists cannot be certain how much radioactive material was present to start with, or whether any had leached out much earlier, or whether the rate of decay has been constant over time. The result can be significant. For example, rocks from the eruption of Mt Ngauruhoe in New Zealand gave various dates up to 3.5 million years, when the lava was known to be sixty years old! There are many examples like this.

Carbon 14 (C-14) dating. Cosmic rays from outer space bombard all living things and form carbon-14 (C-14) atoms. All plants use this C-14, and animals eat the plants. So, everything living has C-14 in it. When something dies, no more C-14 is added, and it slowly disappears—at the rate of half every 5,730 years. This means that beyond 50,000 years there is virtually nothing left to measure. So, if C-14 is present and measurable, the object cannot be many millions of years old.

C-14 has been found in dinosaur fossils—so, they cannot be millions of years old. Carbon-14 has also been found in diamonds and coal that were supposedly more than a billion years old!

Only living things (like plants and animals) take in C-14, therefore the method cannot be used to date rocks. Although C-14 dating is useful for items hundreds or a few thousand years old, it is less reliable for multiple thousands. Also, today C-14 is forming faster than it is decaying, and over the centuries it has varied. Sometimes extra C-14 can be absorbed from other sources like volcanic eruptions and nuclear tests. All this skews results.

There are other dating methods (see the next chapter), but these are the main ones. They all rely on the assumption that changes we see today have been the same for millions of years, but that cannot be proved. And what if the catastrophe that supposedly wiped out the dinosaurs changed a lot more things as well?

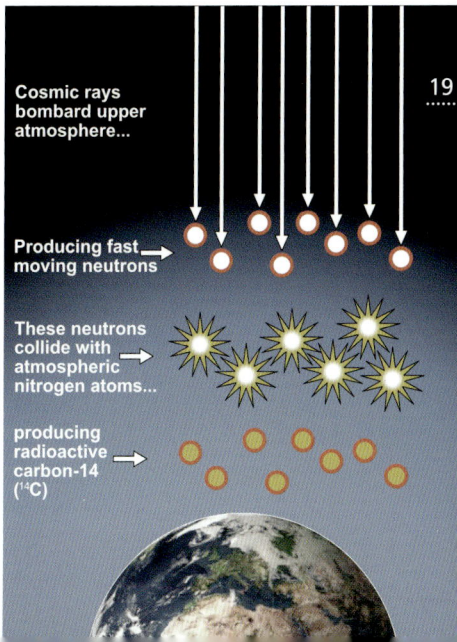

Cosmic rays bombard upper atmosphere...

Producing fast moving neutrons →

These neutrons collide with atmospheric nitrogen atoms... →

producing radioactive carbon-14 (^{14}C) →

10. Big issues— small explanations

Keep in mind that evolution suggests Planet Earth began 4.54 billion years ago and assumes that changes we see today have always been the same.

- The earth's *magnetic field* is decaying at 5% every century. If the earth was even a few tens of thousands of years old, the magnetic field must have been so strong at the start that the earth would have melted. At the present rate the earth must be less than 10,000 years old.

- Rocks contain *helium atoms* from uranium decay. They are so small that they leak rapidly through rock. There is still a lot of helium in rock, so it cannot be billions of years old.

- The *sea* is becoming more *saline (salty)*. Even after millions of years it would be far too saline for any life to survive (think of the Dead Sea in Israel). But the sea is where life supposedly evolved.

- *Comets* are known as 'dirty snowballs' of dust and ice that revolve round the sun. Every time they pass the sun, they lose some of their mass. In even tens or hundreds of thousands of years they would have completely disintegrated.

- *The moon* is slowly moving away from the earth, by about 4 cm each year! Even if the moon was originally part of Planet Earth, it would only need 1.37 billion years to reach where it is. Not the 4.54 billion that is suggested by radiometric dating of moon rock.

- *Erosion of continents.* It is estimated that on average across the globe 60 mm of land is eroded and dumped in the sea every one thousand years. In 2.3 billion years even a continent 93 miles high would now be gone. Even allowing for lava flow from volcanos and uplift from continental plates colliding, the time scale of 4.54 billion years is too great.

- The rate of *population growth*, the evidence of early agriculture and tools, and the evidence of early writing, all point to a young age for humans on Planet Earth, certainly not 200,000 years.

The only answer evolutionists make is to *suggest* big events that changed things. But that destroys the evolutionary view that what we see happening today is the key to what always happened in the past.

Do you want more evidence of a young universe? Head off to: https://creation.com/age-of-the-earth

11. Everybody loves dinosaurs

Did the dinosaurs really become extinct around 65 million years ago before humans were around?

The only way for dating dinosaurs comes from the age of the sedimentary rocks in which their fossils are found—but, as we have seen, that assumes the dating of those rocks is correct.

The word *dinosaur* means 'terrible lizard' and was first used in 1841 by Sir Richard Owen to describe the fossils of the now extinct great sea and land animals. Before that, they were called *dragons*. Richard Owen was an outstanding palaeontologist (those who study fossils).

The best evidence shows dinosaurs and humans were alive at the same time.

- Dragons, as fearsome monsters, are familiar in stories, pictures and images all over the world long before the fossils were ever discovered. Think of the Welsh Dragon. Many Medieval artworks of St George slaying a dragon are easily identified with dinosaurs; for example a *Coelophysis* in a *Book of Hours* (1440) in Castle De Haar (Netherlands) and a *Nothosaurus* in Palau de la Generalitat in Barcelona, Spain (1600). How could people draw so accurately if they had never seen the creatures? There are many ancient images that are clearly those of dinosaurs.

- Two creatures described in the book of Job in the Bible, *Behemoth* and *Leviathan* (Job 40:15–24 and 41:1–34), perfectly fit some of the dinosaurs. *Behemoth* was probably a long-neck-long-tail *sauropod* and *Leviathan* a now-extinct mega-croc like *Sarcosuchus*. Read those two passages. You will be astounded. Do you really think they fit the elephant (look at the tail!) and alligator, as some imagine? Job was one of the earliest books of the Bible, maybe written over 3,000 years ago.

- In 2005 soft tissue, blood vessels and blood cells were found in the bone of a *Tyrannosaurus rex* that supposedly died over 60 million years ago. Many more examples of soft tissue in dinosaur fossils have been found since then, including evidence of proteins and DNA. No scientist, prepared to follow where the hard facts lead, believes soft tissue can survive for 60 million years.

- Carbon-14 has been found in dinosaur bones which, as we saw in dating rocks and fossils, mean they cannot be millions of years old.

If the best evidence is that dinosaurs and humans lived at the same time, why don't scientists abandon the idea of a 65-million-year gap between the alleged extinction of dinosaurs and the arrival of mankind?

Two Sauropods *with intertwined necks in the brass plate on Bishop Bell's tomb 1496 in Carlisle Cathedral, England*

12. Rocky theories

Back in chapter 9 we looked at the way rocks are dated, but there are differing views.

Uniformity (like 'uniform' = all the same) means that all the different rock formations came about gradually over thousands or millions of years by slow changes. That is what we observe today, so it is assumed by many that is how it has always happened.

On the other hand, **Catastrophe** is the view that Planet Earth has been mostly shaped by huge and violent events. Scientists are increasingly accepting the explanation of either asteroid impacts or a flood or both. One view (the Giant Impact Hypothesis) is that around four-and-a-half billion years ago a massive planet slammed into Planet Earth with the force of millions of atomic bombs and created the great limestone mountains. An alternative is the catastrophe of a more recent great flood. Around three-quarters of the surface of the earth is sedimentary rock laid down by water, such as chalk, sandstone, limestone, shale and clay. All over the earth there are layers upon layers of different types of sedimentary rock that show evidence of having been laid down rapidly.

One of the best examples of this is the **Grand Canyon** in Arizona (USA). It is 446 km long, averaging 16 km wide. Many scientists assume it was formed by layers of rock laid down over millions of years. They suggest it then took the Colorado River between 5 and 6 million years to cut through the rock to form the canyon 1.6 km deep. However, there is an alternative explanation illustrated by a more recent event.

In May 1980 the **Mt St Helens** volcano in Washington State (USA) erupted. It was equivalent to 30,000 Hiroshima atom bombs. The eruption reached a temperature of 550 degrees Fahrenheit. A landslide created a wave in Spirit Lake over 182 m high and deposited some 190 m of layers of sediment. On 12 June, 7.5 m of layers were laid and 30 m of solid rock was gouged out to form a canyon. One canyon is one-fortieth in scale of the Grand Canyon. Within a short time, Spirit Lake had a metre of peat in the bed from bark rubbed off the floating log mass—peat is the beginning of coal.

The Mt St Helens canyons may have the appearance of slow erosion—but it was all over in a few days. So, massive layers of sediment forming rock can be laid down very rapidly. Rocks may not be as old as some think.

Layers of sediment forming rock at Mt St Helens (creation.com)

13. Fossils galore

Like dinosaurs, everybody is fascinated by fossils—and so they should be because there are millions of them. They are a significant link with the distant past.

- To become fossils, living creatures (plants, animals, insects) have to be buried rapidly and under great pressure so that all air is squeezed out and body tissue cannot easily decompose. Leave them to rot and you know what happens.

- All fossils, including those of sea (marine) creatures, are found in layers laid down by floodwaters—even on the top of mountains; for example, over 8,000 m in the Himalayas. These present-day mountains were not always so high but were pushed upwards by the tremendous energy on the earth's crust associated with a huge flood.

- In igneous rock (from volcanic ash) occasional outlines of creatures are found, like the humans turned into stone at Pompeii and Herculaneum. But they are not preserved in the same way as fossils in water-lain sedimentary rock.

- Many fossils show all the signs of a rapid covering, such as a fish eating another fish and a two-metre-long *ichthyosaur* giving birth!

- The minute details still seen in many fossils, including the fronds of ferns, the wings of dragonflies, tiny creatures like ants and even fossilised jellyfish, are evidence of rapid burial.

- Many fossils are identical to their modern counterpart—apart from now extinct creatures of course. No change means no evolution.

- Even in the now extinct 'primitive' creatures (like Trilobites and Ammonites), there is evidence of incredible design and engineering, such as complex eyes. It is unbelievable that unplanned, random processes over millions of years resulted in these marvels.

- Vast chalk beds stretch across continents from Europe into Africa and America. These are formed by the compression of many trillions of tiny marine creatures.

All fossils illustrate a sudden death and covering. Is this the result of a massive flood in earth's more recent history?

Remember, in chapter 9 we noted that fossils cannot be dated by C-14 beyond 50,000 years max. So, they are given dates according to the suggested date of the rocks in which they are found. But, in chapter 12 we saw that dating is unreliable.

Fossils of a now extinct fish swallowing a small fish and of a dragonfly

14. Star gazing

Our 'Solar System', centred on our sun and known as the Milky Way, is where all our planets, moons and comets live and it is big—very big.

No one knows how big our galaxy is, but it could be 100,000 light years across. And astronomers think there could be two trillion other galaxies!

So, our Solar System is just one tiny part of outer space. It has eight planets, including Planet Earth, and several dwarf planets, including Pluto. All those planets keep just the right distance from each other as they orbit round the sun so that they don't push each other off course or get burned up by the sun. Together with the stars, they are just where they need to be so that for thousands of years travellers could navigate around Planet Earth and tell the seasons of the year. Their star patterns—think of groups of stars (constellations) like the 'Plough' and 'Orion'—mean they are easy for travellers to find in the sky. And they are just bright enough, and not too bright, to be seen in a night sky.

Now think about Planet Earth

- It is exactly the right distance from the sun to stop the ice caps melting or the oceans evaporating or freezing.

- The rate of the Earth's rotation and the exact tilt of its axis give us our seasons of the year and the length of our days so that we all get a share of the sun's warmth.

- The moon is exactly the right distance from the Earth for its gravitational effect on our tides to keep the oceans moving and fresh. Its cycle from new moon to full moon enabled early humans to mark off the months.

- The Earth's atmosphere has the perfect balance of gas (nitrogen, oxygen, argon and trace gases) for life.
- It has all the minerals and vegetation needed to support life.
- The amount of water, about 70% of the planet's surface, is just right for our human life.
- An ozone layer protects Earth from the harmful ultra violet rays of the sun.

A Big Bang could only fling stuff chaotically into space. No explosion has ever ended up producing a magnificent building full of perfect and detailed interior fittings.

Sir Isaac Newton, possibly the greatest scientist in history, concluded, 'The most beautiful system of the sun, the planets, and comets, could only proceed from the council and dominion of an intelligent and powerful Being' (*Principia Mathematica* 1687).

The galactic plane of the Milky Way seen in the night sky. Source: Wikimedia Commons

15. Look at all the lookalikes

What about Neanderthals as a missing link?

The usual idea is that humans evolved from apes somewhere on the continent of Africa from many scattered areas around two or three hundred thousand years ago all at the same time. No one knows how, and there are many theories. The fact is, in spite of superficial differences like skin, eye and hair colour, all over the world humans (*Homo sapiens*) all have the same genetic code and can breed with each other. Humans cannot breed with apes.

Neanderthals from Eurasia and Denisovans from Asia were supposedly 'ancient man' that became extinct around 40,000 years ago. At one time, Neanderthals were thought to be the missing link between apes and us. But no longer. Their brain case is slightly different from modern humans, and their skeleton was more robust and thick-set than in most people today. However, it is now agreed that they interbred with 'modern' humans and our DNA has been found in both. So, they are clearly members of the human race and not a separate sub-human animal. In fact, probably many of us have a bit of Neanderthal DNA in us!

By the way, DNA is so fragile, it cannot last even for 40,000 years. Scientists studying extinct moa birds leg bones found that 75% of the DNA information is lost every 1,000 years.

Some recent research has caused a stir. In 2018, two scientists from the University of Basle in Switzerland, Mark Stoeckle and David Thaler, researched into the 'DNA barcodes' of humans and concluded that we all began from two parents around 200,000 years ago. They concluded that the same is true of virtually all animals. Afraid that they might have undermined evolution, they insist they are still fully committed to Darwin's view of origins and 'we do not propose a single Adam and Eve. We do not propose any catastrophic events'. Apparently, we all started from an original pair, but not Adam and Eve!

All this means that, unless you dislike humanity, there is no such thing as the prejudice of 'racism', because although across the world there are many languages, cultures and customs, all humans belong to just one race—we are all one human family descended from the first pair.

Artist's impression of a Neanderthal

16. The Big Flood?

In chapter 10 we saw that most scientists accept that at some point in earth's history there was a terrible catastrophe.

A Big Flood would account for the fact that all fossils are found in sedimentary rock—rock laid down by water. The Bible book of Genesis records that the whole of Planet Earth was once completely covered with water. Genesis 6:7,17 reads:

> 'I will wipe from the face of the earth the human race I have created—and with them the animals, the birds and the creatures that move along the ground … I am going to bring floodwaters on the earth to destroy all life under the heavens, every creature that has the breath of life in it. Everything on earth will perish.'

Notice how devastating this was: 'The waters rose and increased greatly on the earth … all the high mountains under the entire heavens were covered. The waters rose and covered the mountains to a depth of more than twenty feet.' 'High mountains' may have been little more than great hills at that time; the huge forces of the Flood would create today's high mountains. That was certainly a catastrophe! God also said, 'Never again will all life be destroyed by the waters of a flood; never again will there be a flood to destroy the earth' (Genesis 7:18–20; 9:11).

So, it can't refer to local floods of which there are still many.

It's a fact that on every continent (except Antarctica) from ancient times on, there are stories of an earth-wide flood. Some are wacky, but some are a bit like the Bible's account. Doesn't that suggest that there really was a great, catastrophic flood?

Significantly, Jesus and his disciple Peter believed in a planet-wide flood. Jesus in Matthew 24:38–39, 'In the days before the flood, people were eating and drinking, marrying and giving in marriage, up to the day Noah entered the ark; and they knew nothing about what would happen until the flood came and took them all away'. And Peter in 2 Peter 2:5; 3:6, 'God did not spare the ancient world when he brought the flood on its ungodly people … By these waters also the world of that time was deluged and destroyed.'

In Kentucky (USA) a full-size ark has been built on the dimensions recorded in the Bible to show that it was possible for Noah and the animals to live on it during the Flood

17. The best kept secret

Why aren't these challenges to the theory of evolution openly discussed?

The popular acceptance of the theory of evolution in the middle of the nineteenth century encouraged a growing disbelief in the existence of God in our society.

The widely accepted position among many scientists is that evolution explains everything—well, almost everything—so God is not needed. Do you remember the *naturalism* in chapter 2—the belief that everything that happens now and happened in the past is the result of natural causes that scientists can explain?

If theories are presented as fact for long enough, eventually everybody believes them. It's like 'fake news'. Even most scientists believe the theory of evolution is fact and never bother to question it. Most people are like that. When you have accepted a position for a long time and then someone comes along with strong arguments against it, you are very reluctant to change your position because you lose credibility among your friends or colleagues. No one wants to be the odd one out. Many scientific journals refuse to publish excellent articles by top-level scientists who believe in a God of creation. And some even lose their job if they question evolution.

Here is the reason for this best kept secret

If we admit that the long, slow, chance process of evolution following an explosion randomly flinging stuff everywhere, doesn't fit either with good science or sound reason, we are left with the strong possibility of God.

For many, the idea that all things came into being by the creating power of an almighty and all wise God is not welcome. So, they must try to explain everything another way—and any arguments against their faith in *naturalism* must be dismissed. At all costs, we cannot allow God. Many who believe in evolution admit this. Not all scientists who believe in evolution are atheists, but they have accepted the same agenda.

Think about it: no one can deny the *possibility* of 'God' because there is zero scientific *proof* that there is no God. Atheism is a matter of personal belief, not science. But if our personal faith in *naturalism* limits our ability to consider the possibility of God, that's not good science.

When a university professor suggests the universe is 'an elaborate and engaging rearrangement of nothing', perhaps unintentionally he admits to a miracle, because no scientist believes that something can come from absolutely nothing—unless there is a miracle!

To challenge evolution is good science.

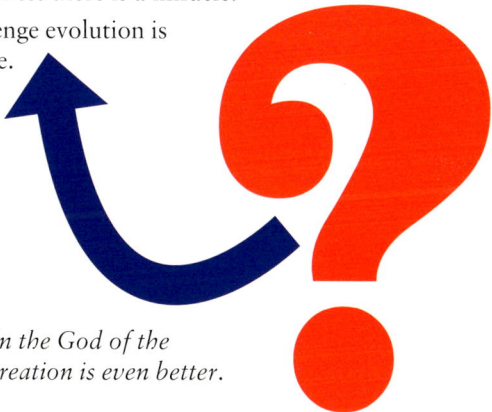

To believe in the God of the miracle of creation is even better.

18. A perfect alternative

Is there nothing better than a universe of billions of years of unimaginable and unbelievable chance coincidences with a future of an empty nothingness?

Darwin himself admitted that how life originated is 'a hopeless enquiry' that possibly would never be resolved. Suppose we don't listen to him and instead of beginning half way through the story of beginnings we go back to the real start?

Since there must be something that always existed, and evolution has no idea what, the Christian response is both sensible and logical: An eternal, self-existing Creator began everything, and he has told us that he did it. The Bible begins like this: 'In the beginning God created the heavens and the earth' (Genesis 1:1).

Seven times in Genesis 1 we read 'And God said' and each time a new part of creation was made. This is the answer to something out of nothing. God alone can do that. It was a miracle. The amazing beauty, harmony, design and detail that we see all around us, should lead us to only one conclusion: God made this.

Jesus healed people from terrible deformities and illnesses instantly; in a moment he created bread and fish for a great crowd of people; and he raised people from the dead. So, it's not strange to believe that when Genesis chapter one says 'God created', he meant just that.

- It is sensible science that where there is design there is always a designer.

- It agrees with the stack of evidence that Planet Earth is not billions (or millions) of years old.
- The Bible account of Adam and Eve answers the question how the human race got started.
- The account of Babel in Genesis 11 explains how the human race scattered, and languages developed.
- The great Flood in the time of Noah fits the fact that around three quarters of our planet is covered by sedimentary rock laid down by water. Most scientists believe there was a catastrophic something in the past.

When you bring a Creator God into the origin of everything, it all makes sense—logically and scientifically. A universe of design and order points to a Creator, and a Creator with a good plan for the future.

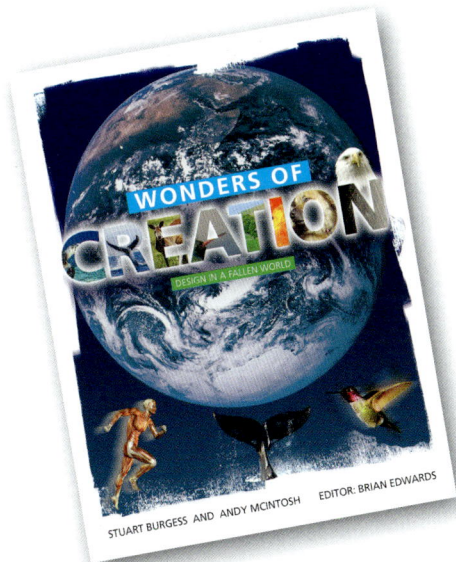

WONDERS OF CREATION

DESIGN IN A FALLEN WORLD

STUART BURGESS AND ANDY MCINTOSH   EDITOR: BRIAN EDWARDS

19. Who believes that?

Many important scientists of history believed in God as the Creator of the universe—and many scientists still do.

The Royal Society was established in 1660 and is the oldest scientific society in the world. Many of its founder members believed the Bible and its account of creation. Its charter included: 'For the glory of God the Creator.' Sir Isaac Newton was its President from 1703 to 1727 and he claimed: 'Atheism is so senseless.'

In 1865 over seven hundred scientists, including eighty-six Fellows of the Royal Society, signed *The Declaration of Students of the Natural and Physical Sciences*. They opposed Darwin and affirmed their confidence in the Bible as a statement of creation. It began:

'We, the undersigned Students of the natural Sciences, desire to express our sincere regret, that researches into scientific truth are perverted by some in our own times into occasion for casting doubt upon Truth and Authenticity of the Holy Scriptures.'

They claimed that if a scientist's *interpretation* of his results *appears* to be a contradiction of the Scriptures, he should not 'presumptuously affirm' that his own conclusions must be right and the Bible wrong.

Sadly, as we have seen, a belief in evolution limits freedom for scientific thinking. However, a belief in God and a designed and ordered universe is the sure foundation for scientific research. Here are a few of many important scientists who believed in God as Creator. It was their belief in the Creator's ordered design that was the basis for their scientific research.

Johannes Kepler (b. 1571). Among the first to track the true positions and motions of the planets. He is known as one of the founders of modern science.

Isaac Newton (b. 1642). Possibly the most famous scientist of all time who gave us the law of gravity, plus calculus and much else.

John Flamstead (b. 1646). Founder of the Greenwich Observatory and first Astronomer Royal.

Michael Faraday (b. 1791). Inventor of electromagnetism and the generator.

'All variety of created objects which represent order and life in the universe could happen only by the willful reasoning of its original Creator, whom I call the "Lord God"'
— Isaac Newton

James Joule (b. 1818). The first to show the importance of thermodynamics and much more. He showed the precise order in the universe.

William Thomson (**Lord Kelvin**, b. 1824). Invented the international system of absolute temperature.

Joseph Lister (b. 1827). Introduced antiseptic surgery.

James Maxwell (b. 1831). One of the greatest scientists of all time. His pioneering work in electromagnetism is the basis for all our technology from cell phones to satellites. He strongly opposed evolution.

Across the world today, there are many thousands of excellent scientists who believe in God as the Creator of the universe. Lord Kelvin once wrote: 'Do not be afraid of being free-thinkers. If you think strongly enough you will be forced by science to the belief in God.'

20. Does it really matter?

Keeping secret the alternative to evolution hinders real science, but more importantly it prevents us from listening to the God who created everything.

We can enjoy creation even more because 'the whole earth is full of God's glory' (Isaiah 6:3). The Christian worships. The best the atheist can do is to say 'Wow!'

Without God, there can be no purpose in the universe. Everything is the result of blind chance and therefore without meaning. That includes us. If we are no more than molecules and atoms we have no real purpose. Our lives lead to nothingness: it's called oblivion. And that leads to despair.

Without God, there is no clear definition of right and wrong. It's all a matter of what society decides. But society is constantly changing. In the eighteenth century society thought slavery was right and gay relationships were wrong—so why have these changed places today?

Without God, there is no final justice. In the end, the bad guys are no worse off than the good guys. And for those who have a life of painful suffering, there is no hope in the future either. In fact, there is no future.

However, if there is a Creator, we might expect him to give us instructions on how best to live—and he has.

The Bible, like creation, is not chaotically thrown together, but all through it is revealing that God has a plan for Planet Earth (past, present and future) and it centres on Jesus Christ coming here.

If you read the first few chapters of the Bible you have the beginning of everything.

- We read of God's perfectly designed creation, exactly right for human life.
- God's plan for harmony in relationships by marriage between one man and one woman.
- His special relationship with the human race.
- We also read how badly things went wrong when the first humans left God out, and what he has planned to do to make things right.

Even more important is the fact that when Jesus came onto Planet Earth, he not only taught us why he came and how we should live but he showed us what God is like and promised a good future for Planet Earth and for all who follow him. The Bible teaches us the purpose and meaning of our lives so that our empty nothingness can become a life of hope for ever. That is what the Bible is all about.

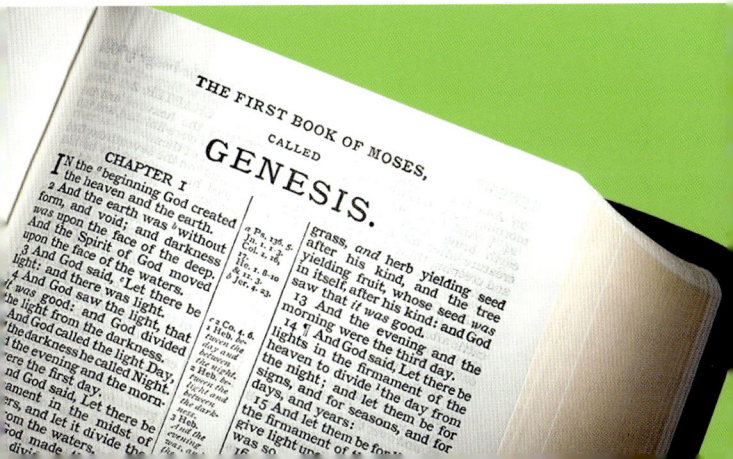

There are five more
Is it True? **booklets**
just like this one

(all obtainable from Day One
Publications — details on back cover)

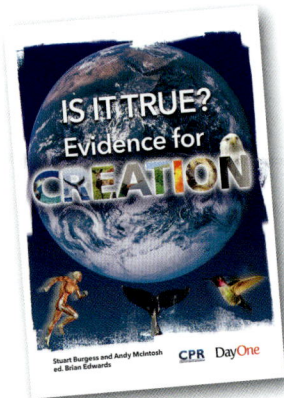

IS IT TRUE?
Evidence for
CREATION

Stuart Burgess and Andy McIntosh
ed. Brian Edwards

CPR DayOne

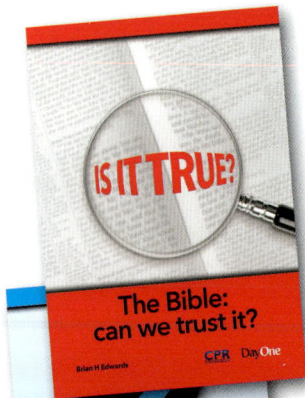

IS IT TRUE?

The Bible:
can we trust it?

Brian H Edwards

CPR DayOne

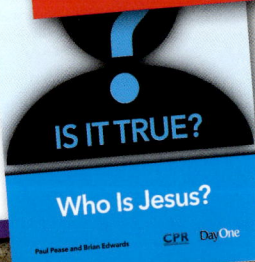

IS IT TRUE?

Who Is Jesus?

Paul Pease and Brian Edwards

CPR DayOne

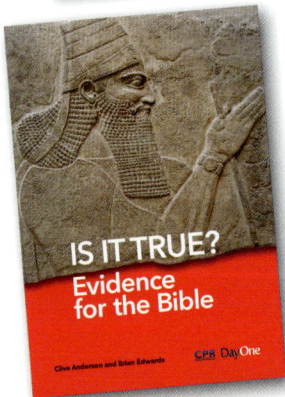

IS IT TRUE?
Evidence
for the Bible

Clive Anderson and Brian Edwards

CPR DayOne

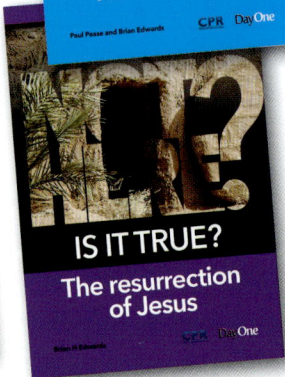

IS IT TRUE?

The resurrection
of Jesus

Brian H Edwards

CPR DayOne

A beautifully illustrated large format book by two leading scientists and university professors.
It covers all the subjects dealt with in this booklet including:

- Evidence for creation
- Irreducible complexity
- The uniqueness of humans
- Dinosaurs
- Rocks and fossils
- Starlight and planets
- The marks of creation in beauty and mathematics

... and much more

WONDERS OF CREATION

DESIGN IN A FALLEN WORLD

2022 EDITION

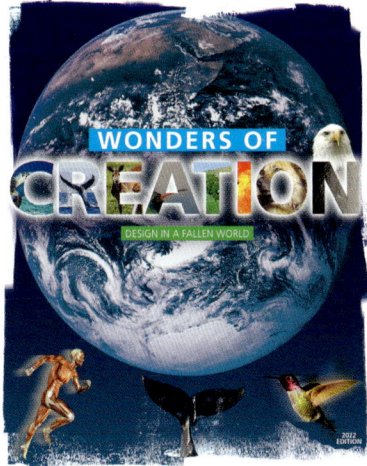

STUART BURGESS AND ANDY MCINTOSH   EDITOR: BRIAN EDWARDS

Stuart Burgess has held scientific posts in engineering and design in Cambridge, Bristol and the USA. He was lead scientist for the design of the solar array for the ENVISAT earth observation satellite and for the chain drive of the record-breaking track bikes in the 2016 Rio Olympics.

Andy McIntosh is a Professor in Mathematics and Thermodynamics and has held scientific posts in Leeds and the USA. He invented a spray technology used in pharmaceutics, aerosols and fire extinguishers.

Here are three books on this subject by Professor Burgess. Deep science easy to understand.

The origin of man
The image of an ape or the image of God?

He made the stars also
What the Bible says about the stars
Stuart Burgess

Hallmarks of design
Evidence of purposeful design and beauty in nature
Stuart Burgess

The above are available from DayOne.co.uk

Untold Secrets of Planet Earth—Dire Dragons
by **Vance Nelson** who holds degrees in theology and biology.
A fascinatingly illustrated hard cover book clearly revealing that dinosaurs lived at the same time as humans.
ISBN 978-0-98688-215-9   Available from Creation.com

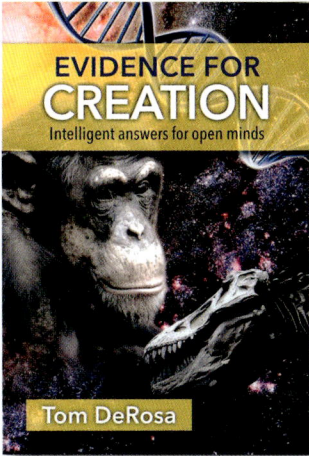

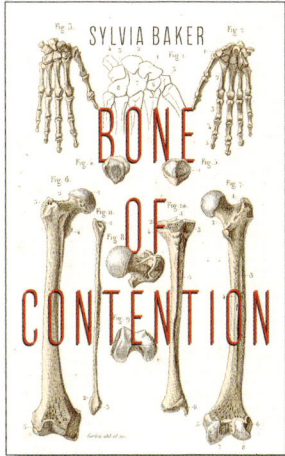

Do you want to dig deeper?
Here are two readable books to take you further
into the subjects introduced in this booklet.

Tom DeRosa is Founder and Executive Director of the Creation Studies Institute. He holds a master's degree in Education and has written widely on this subject.

Sylvia Baker has a degree in Biology, a master's in Radiation Biology and a doctorate in Education.

Both can be obtained from
Creation Ministries International
Creation.com

IS IT TRUE?
Evolution

The origin of the universe and life on Planet Earth has fascinated humanity for thousands of years. The incredible detail, beauty and order, and how everything works, is mind-blowing even to a casual observer of everything around them. But where did it all come from—and when, and how?

Early in the nineteenth century many began to study the subject in depth and they came up with ideas that slowly crystallised into a theory known as 'evolution'—that everything happened slowly from small beginnings to the complex universe that we know today. Since those early days, many scientists have concluded that we now know for certain what was once suggested as ideas. 'Evolution' is assumed to be a fact that no one can question.

But is it all as simple as that? Do the many ideas behind evolution always fit the known facts that science reveals of the world and universe around us? Is there an alternative, and if so, why is it not openly discussed?

This little booklet sets out some thought-provoking challenges to what many assume is unquestionably true.

Day One Publications
Ryelands Road Leominster HR6 8NZ
Email: sales@dayone.co.uk
www.dayone.co.uk
© +44 (0) 1568 613 740
© Toll Free 888 329 6630 (North America)

ISBN 978-1-84625-776-6